Tell me

What children really want to know about bodies, sex and emotions

Katharina von der Gat

GECK

Katharina von der Gathen has made a career in sex education. She conducts school workshops for children and teenagers. The questions featured in this book come from a sex education project with students around nine or ten years old.

Anke Kuhl works as an illustrator in the LABOR studio in Frankfurt. She has illustrated many books, including *Alles Familie!*, which won the German Youth Literature Prize, and *Alle Kinder: Ein ABC der Schadenfreude.*

What is this book about?

This is a book of questions from many different children.
They wrote down their questions about bodies, puberty, love
and sexuality and anonymously put them into a box with the
promise that I would answer every question. A number of
them—99!—have been collected here.

Illustrator Anke Kuhl has drawn lively, funny and thoughtful
pictures to go with my answers. The questions are in no particular
order, so you can read the book backwards if you like or dip in
and out. You can also look up questions in the back of the book.

Some of these questions could have many different answers.
You will relate to some more than others. If you feel concerned
about anything relating to your body or your feelings, it's
important to get help—and there are lots of places to go for
more information about questions raised in this book. Talk to an
adult you can trust—maybe a parent, family doctor, teacher or
school nurse—contact community organizations and helplines
and look at reputable websites. Start your web search with public
organizations that work in the areas of children's health and
reproduction.

My thanks to all the children who have asked me questions
over the years. Without your curiosity, trust and openness,
this book would not exist.

Katharina von der Gathen

Johanni – for you!
And for you: Andi, Lotta, Karline, Emil, Franz
K.v.d.G.

1

What's so important about bodies anyway?

1 What's so important about bodies anyway?

Each of us has our own unique body. We can move it, look at it and feel it. But sometimes our bodies do things we can't control. They suddenly grow, or start to itch somewhere, or even get sick. Bodies are always changing.

The world we live in has a lot to say about bodies. There are expectations about how our bodies should look and behave. Our cultures can present a narrow view of what's "normal," but people come in infinite variations.

You only get one body in this life, and you and your feelings are right inside it. That's why it's important to get to know your body and how it works. You'll see what a remarkable thing it is.

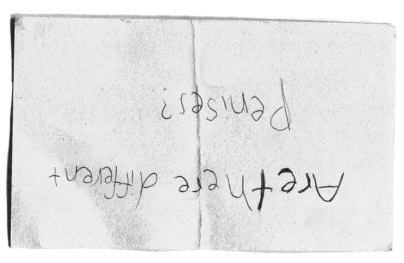

Are there different
Penises?

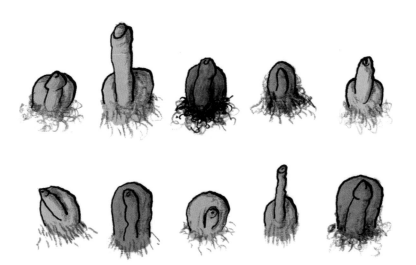

2 Are there different penises?

As many as there are people! You can't choose the penis you're born with. Some are long, some are thin, some short and thick, others large... Penises come in all shapes and sizes. Just like noses, each one looks different.

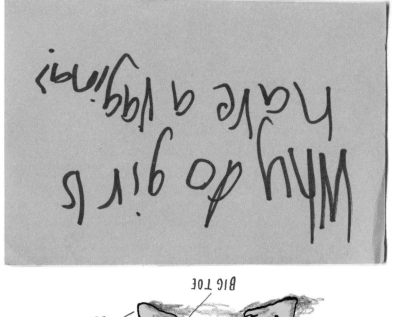

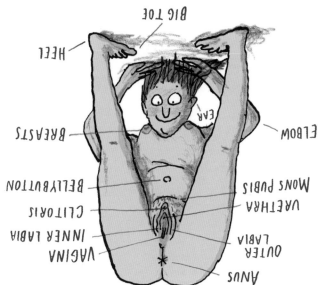

3 Why do girls have a vagina?

Nature has arranged things cleverly. Some people have a vagina and others have a penis. (Others can be intersex, but that's a different topic.) Human beings need these two organs to reproduce.

People use the word vagina to mean what you can see between the legs of women and girls, but it's actually a vulva, which has several parts:

- the outer and inner labia or lips
- at the front, under a kind of "hood," is the clitoris
- further back is the urethra exit, where urine comes out of a small hole
- and behind that is the entrance to the vagina.

To be exact, the vagina is the finger-length tunnel that leads from the vulva to the uterus.

Menstrual blood comes out of the vagina. A baby also comes into the world through the vagina.

4

4 How long is a penis?

Each one is different, so it's not possible to say exactly how long a penis is. Many penises are pretty small at first glance. But once a penis swells, it can suddenly look quite big. Scientists have measured many different penises. They've concluded that the stiff penis of an adult is about 14 cm / 5½ in. long, on average. However, anything from 5–25 cm / 2–10 in. is considered a normal length. (A penis can keep growing until you are about 20 years old.)

5

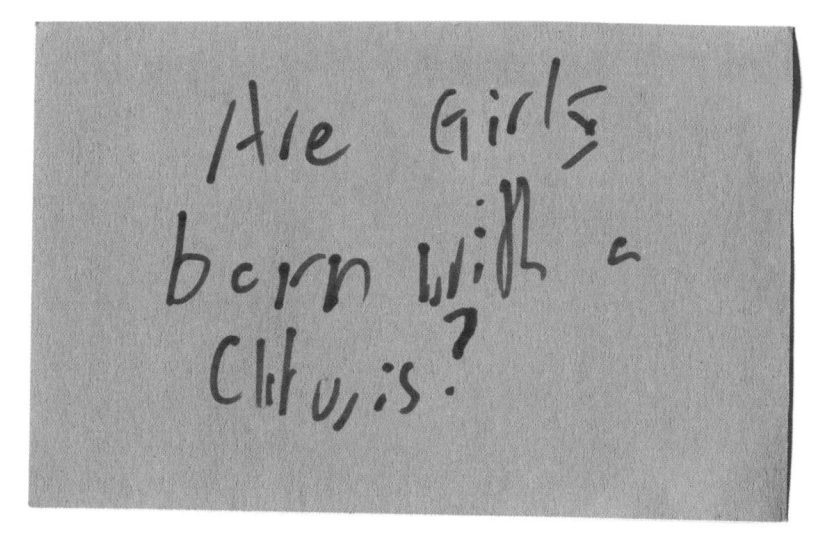

Are Girls born with a Clitoris?

5 Are girls born with a clitoris?

Most of them are! The clitoris is a body part whose only purpose is to give feelings of pleasure. It feels like a small nub at the top of the vulva, sometimes hidden by a hood of skin. Just like the tip of a penis, it is very sensitive to touch. Even little babies can feel pleasure when they rub their clitoris.

9

6 How does a man get a vagina if he had a penis?

Most people are born with either male or female genitals, but body parts and who a person feels themself to be are not always the same thing.

Sometimes a baby can be born with a penis and they are told they are a boy, but they are actually a girl. They and their parents might only come to realize things are different for them over a period of time. Their "boy" body doesn't feel right and they start to identify as a trans girl.

In early childhood, this is sometimes not too big a deal, but as the girl gets older, it can become more difficult to have this body that doesn't feel like their own. They might decide to talk to a doctor about changing their body with artificial hormones. These can stop body changes like growing a beard and start other changes, like forming breasts. Later, some people choose to undergo a complicated operation that can form a vagina from a penis.

It is same for a person born with the parts of a girl who is actually a boy. People who identify as a different gender than the one they are born with are called transgender.

7

What Are the Bags bch.nd the Penis?

7 What are the bags behind the penis?

Strictly speaking, there's only one bag, called a scrotum. Inside that are two halves, and two little balls called testicles. Children's testicles are about the size of a marble. Later they grow to the size of a walnut. Testicles can move around quite a bit. Sometimes they go so far up that you might think the scrotum is empty. But most of the time they quickly slip back down. The testicles are where sperm cells are made. Sperm cells are one half of what's needed to make a baby. The scrotum is a great air conditioner. It would be too warm for sperm inside the body, so the scrotum hangs outside. It can stretch in the heat and hang even lower. And if things get too cold for the sperm cells, the scrotum shrinks to keep the testicles close to the warm body.

how many sperm
does a man
make

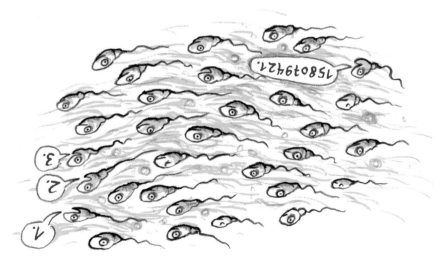

8   How many sperm does a man make?

In puberty, the testicles start producing sperm cells. Quite a few—in fact, several hundred million a day. We call them sperm. The testicles are like small factories that constantly produce and store new sperm and replace them when they're no longer fresh. This factory stays in production from puberty right through old age.

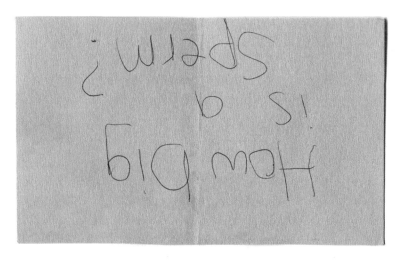

How big
is a
sperm?

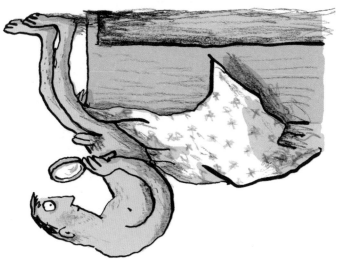

9 How big is a sperm?

Sperm cells are so small you can't see them with the naked eye. Sperm can come out of the body when someone ejaculates. Ejaculation happens at the most intense sexual stimulation, and then a whitish liquid squirts or dribbles out of the penis (about a teaspoonful). The sperm cells (about 400 million of them) swim in this liquid, called semen. Under a microscope they look like little tadpoles. Each sperm is very, very tiny. An egg cell is much bigger by comparison—about the size of the dot on an i.

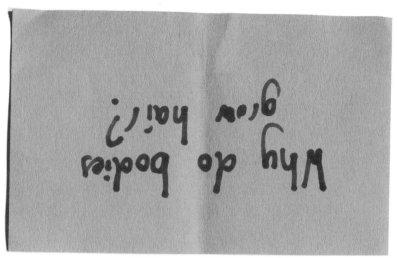

Why do bodies grow hair?

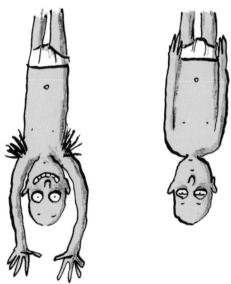

10 Why do bodies grow hair?

We can see from the many hairs all over our bodies that our ancestors were animals with fur. Humans have lost most of this furry coat, but the hair we still have helps us. The hair on our head keeps us warm. The hair in our armpits helps sweat to evaporate. Eyebrows and eyelashes protect our eyes from injury. And the many tiny hairs all over our bodies help us feel touch better, such as when someone gently strokes our skin. Hair on the legs, in the armpits and around the vagina and penis only starts to grow at the age of about nine to twelve. This is a visible sign of growing up. Adult scent clings to this hair.

Everyone has this hair on their bodies—some are hairier, others have less hair. Like everything to do with our bodies, there's a lot of variation between people. Some adults think that hair around their armpits, vagina and penis is fine. Others shave this hair or pluck it out.

11 How do voices break?

In puberty, it sometimes sounds as if a boy's voice is "broken." It can suddenly become hoarse, or high, or sometimes seem especially loud.

During puberty, hormones cause the body to grow sporadically in all sorts of ways. The larynx and vocal cords, which allow us to make sound in our throat, double their size. But the surrounding muscles don't grow at the same rate. All these changes inside the throat and face can make the voice crack and squeak. After a few months, everything settles down, and you'll hear a new, much deeper voice. Many boys like this very much.

Girls, too, get a deeper voice in puberty, but it's not so noticeable because the vocal cords and larynx don't grow so much.

What's a hormone?

12 What's a hormone?

Hormones are chemicals made in the body. They control all of its important functions—growth, digestion, temperature and even feelings. When you reach puberty, your body begins to produce special sex hormones that make the whole body grow and change. Male hormones cause hair to grow on the chin, under the arms and around the penis, and make ejaculation possible. Female hormones cause hair to grow under the arms and around the vulva, cause the breasts to grow and menstruation to begin. Every person has both male and female hormones—each of us has our own unique mix. Sometimes emotions run pretty crazy, too. And it's all because of hormones.

13

Why does puberty happen, and why does it last so long?

13 Why does puberty happen, and why does it last so long?

Puberty is the shift from childhood to adulthood. During this time a lot changes, inside and outside of the body, as well as in a person's thoughts and feelings. Because these are big changes that happen slowly, puberty lasts a long time. People reach puberty at different times. Some feel the physical changes when they're eight or nine. Others might be fourteen and still waiting for puberty to start. Usually females reach puberty a little earlier than males.

why is it
called puberty?

14 Why is it called puberty?

The word puberty comes from Latin. The original word is *pubertas*, which means sexual maturity. So, just as an apple on the tree becomes more beautiful and red-cheeked as it ripens, children who reach puberty are maturing and becoming ripe for life as an adult—ready for love, and for having children of their own if they choose to.

Is it possible not to go through puberty?

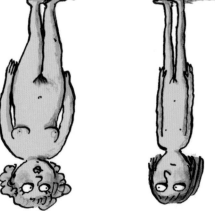

LENA, 14 years   SUSIE, 11 years

15 Is it possible not to go through puberty?

Sooner or later, most children experience puberty. They grow and their bodies change. They start to grow hair on their bodies, have their first ejaculation or get their period. All of this is triggered by hormones.

In very rare cases a child's body doesn't produce hormones at puberty. These people can get medical help.

Some children are afraid they'll never reach puberty, others don't want to change at all. Don't worry. With patience and grit—and if things feel serious, with help—you'll get through this tumultuous time just fine.

16

How do you know
when you're
a grownup?

16 How do you know when you're a grownup?

It's easy to recognize the outward signs of growing up. Your body changes, hair sprouts in new places, your breasts or penis get bigger, your voice sounds deeper, you get your period or start to ejaculate. At some point it doesn't feel right to call yourself a child any more. Your own opinions feel more important, you want to try new things and decide for yourself what's right and what's good for you. There might be more arguments with adults.

As exhausting as it is for everyone, you know you're growing up and want to take responsibility for yourself. As a teenager, you are well on your way to being "grownup." There's still a way to go, though—the brain keeps growing until a person's mid-twenties.

Still, none of that means you can never be childish or silly any more.

Why is it embarrasing to see someone's ass es penis or vagina?

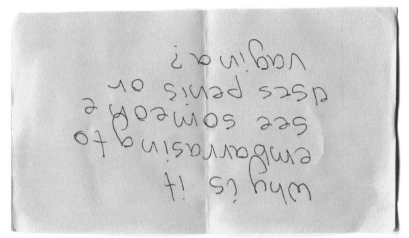

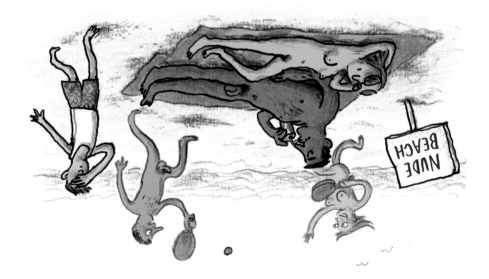

17 Why is it embarrassing to see someone else's penis or vagina?

Little children love to run around naked. But bigger kids can start to feel self-conscious and that being naked is something personal. And even if the whole family runs around naked at home, nobody does that at the mall. This embarrassment can be a good thing, because it helps you learn to take care of yourself.

As an adult, everyone has their own sense of modesty. Some people like to go to the sauna naked, while others will only get changed behind a locked bathroom door. There are different rules in different countries and cultures. For some communities, being naked in everyday life is quite normal. Elsewhere, people feel uncomfortable seeing someone with bare arms or no head covering.

18 Why do I get a stiff penis when I hear people talk about sex?

Blame your brain. It sends instructions to the rest of the body. Sometimes, when you think about sex or a sexual situation, blood collects in your penis, which grows bigger and a bit harder and might stick out. This is called an erection. You can get an erection in other situations, too, such as when you really need to pee, when something is especially exciting, when you dream, or for no reason at all. For many people this happens several times a day. It can't always be controlled. At some point, the blood slowly flows away and the penis softens and hangs down again.

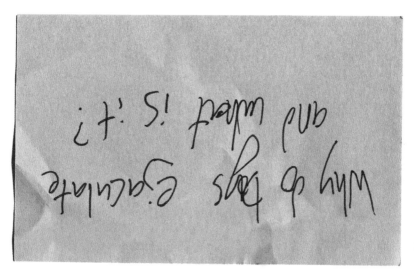

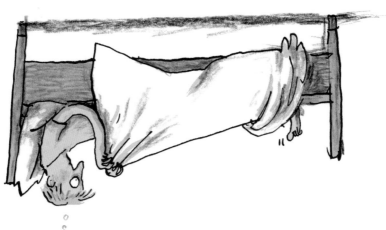

19 Why do boys ejaculate and what is it?

Everyone who has a penis will experience an ejaculation at some point. If you are sexually excited and the feeling becomes very strong, a whitish, sticky liquid comes out of the stiff penis. This liquid contains many millions of sperm cells. This is called an ejaculation. At that moment, for a few seconds, you might have a wonderful feeling of pleasure. This is called an orgasm.

An ejaculation can come when you masturbate, or at night when you're asleep and don't even notice it, or while you're having a wonderful sexy dream. When you wake in the morning, your pajama pants might be damp. No problem, you can just wash them.

Why do you
bleed from
your vagina?

20 Why do you bleed from your vagina?

At some point during puberty, girls start to get menstrual periods. This is called *menstruation* or a *period*. The blood during menstruation comes from the uterus at the top of the vagina.

This process is technically about the body preparing to become pregnant.

Females produce egg cells inside their bodies. Each month an egg cell travels to the uterus, which has prepared a soft mucous-membrane lining. If the egg becomes fertilized and needs a snug nest—if a person becomes pregnant—the egg rests in this lining. It is now an embryo and will grow into a baby that is nourished by this special lining in the uterus. Most months the egg is not fertilized, so the mucous membrane is not needed. It flows and drips out of the vagina, along with a bit of blood. The amount of liquid is actually very small—usually two or three tablespoons over a few days.

After you start menstruating, you will get your period and bleed from your vagina for a few days about every four weeks.

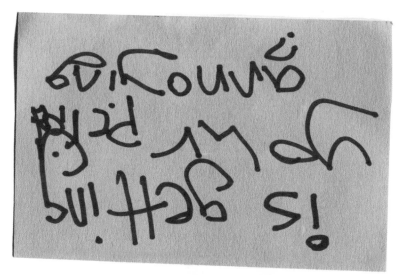

21 Is getting your period annoying?

A lot of new things happen when you get your period. You can try out the different methods available to soak up the blood so it doesn't get on your clothes—pads, tampons, menstrual cups, special absorbent underwear—and figure out how to deal with them. You might have sore breasts, or get belly or back cramps when you menstruate, as the uterus contracts to get rid of the built-up mucous membrane. And sometimes you might feel emotional changes. Some days you just want to be left alone.

All this can be pretty annoying at times. But it isn't always so, and everyone experiences their period differently. You can keep doing everything you normally do when you have your period—swimming, exercizing, whatever feels comfortable. Some people feel proud and happy to get their period, because it's a sign of becoming an adult.

ABRACADABRA, SPROUT, SPROUT, COME OUT!

22

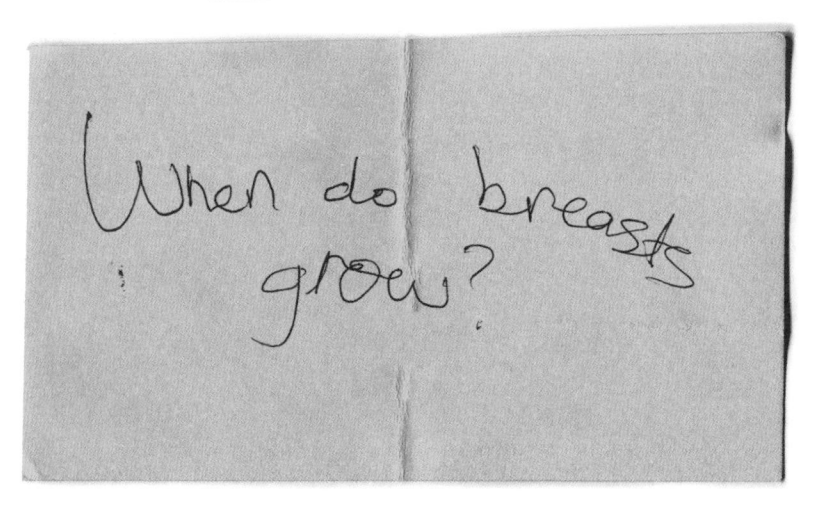

22 When do breasts grow?

Some people can already feel their breasts beginning to grow at the age of nine or ten. For others, this doesn't start until they're thirteen or fourteen. Breasts aren't full-sized until the whole body is fully grown (usually in the late teens), and they can change size through life when you gain or lose weight. Sometimes breasts don't develop evenly, and one might be slightly bigger than the other for a time.

why do-breasts
hang down

PUSH-UP BRA →

23 Why do breasts hang down?

When breasts begin to grow at the start of puberty, they don't usually hang down. (Although this depends on size—the bigger the breasts, the more likely they are to hang lower.) Sometimes this happens as women get older, because breasts are mostly made up of connective tissues and fat, rather than muscle, and the tissue stretches. There are many different types of breasts in any case—pointy, plump, flat, round, wide. And not all end up hanging down. Many women wear a bra to support their breasts.

Why do you get pimples?

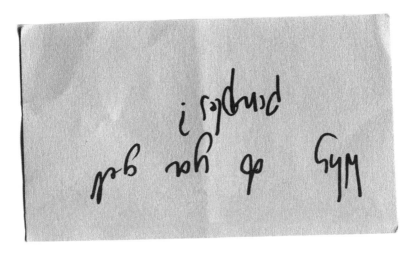

24 Why do you get pimples?

Many children get pimples when they reach puberty. Hormones are the reason once again. They ensure that the body develops from a child into an adult. They also cause fat to be produced in the many tiny pores of the skin. This fat can clog the pores, and sometimes these spots become infected. These are pimples. You can actually get pimples all through your life, because the body constantly produces new hormones.

is it weird going through puberty

25

25 Is it weird going through puberty?

Weird is a good word for it when you realize how much goes on in puberty that's new and different. Girls get their periods for the first time and boys have their first ejaculation. Your body is slowly becoming an adult body. You don't really feel like a kid any more, but you're not treated as an adult, either. Weirdly fantastic and weirdly stupid, weirdly exciting and weirdly self-conscious, weirdly funny and weirdly desperate. For each person puberty feels different, day by day. And that really is weird!

Why do people
feel desire?

26 Why do people feel desire?

Everyone knows what it's like to feel desire—the desire for ice cream, the desire to move or to be tickled, the desire to cuddle. When you feel desire, you want something that you like and that makes you feel good.

Adults and teenagers might also feel a desire to have sex. Nature has set this up well, because sex can result in babies. Sex of all kinds is also an important way that humans form social bonds, so desire for sex is part of human evolution.

Some people don't feel sexual desire and that's fine, too.

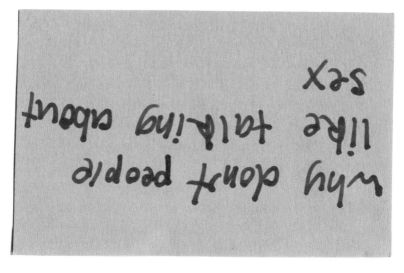

why don't people like talking about sex

YOU'VE HAD SEX AT LEAST ONCE!

NEVER!

27 Why don't people like talking about sex?

For most people, sex is natural, but there are some things that you only want to talk to certain people about (such as a best friend). Sexuality is a topic a lot of people feel shy about discussing with anyone other than their partner. So if you ask someone if, when or how they had sex, you might not get an answer.

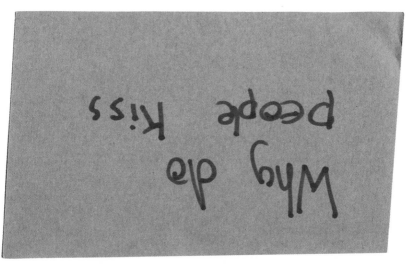

Why do
people kiss

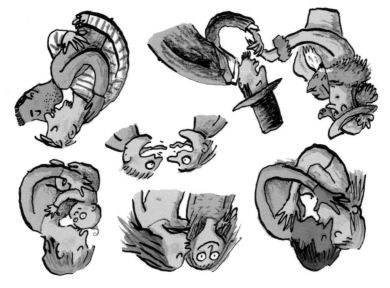

28 Why do people kiss?

If you want to be very close to a person, kissing usually comes into it. Around the mouth and on the lips the skin is very thin with many nerve endings, making it very sensitive to touch. A kiss is a way to let someone feel your love and affection. There are many different kinds of kisses. The kiss between parents and children, the kiss to greet friends, a deep kiss between two lovers, or a formal kiss on the hand. Everyone can decide for themselves whether they want to kiss or not.

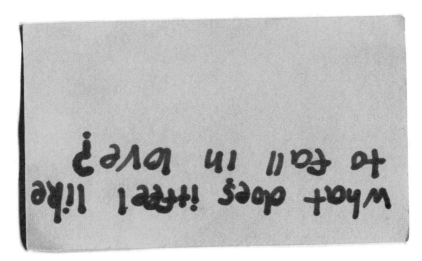

What does it feel like
to fall in love?

29 What does it feel like to fall in love?

Falling in love feels different for every person. Maybe you can't think of anything except the person you love. Maybe your heart beats wildly and you get butterflies in your stomach whenever that person is around. Maybe you're excited and can barely eat. Or falling in love might feel completely different. You'll know it when you do feel it, though, because falling in love is a strong emotion. And it's even better when the other person feels the same way.

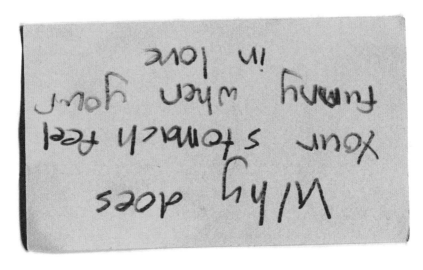

Why does
your stomach feel
funny when you're
in love

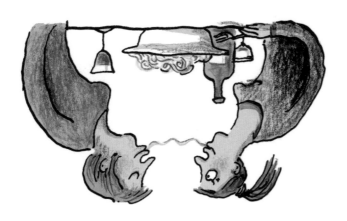

30 Why does your stomach feel funny when you're in love?

Love and the stomach. What do they have to do with one another? Anyone who has fallen madly in love knows what happens in your stomach. You get butterflies. Sometimes you feel almost sick with excitement, or you can't eat. "The way to the heart is through the stomach" is a saying you may have heard. This means you can show love with food—but there are lots of different ways to show love. Somehow the stomach and emotions are closely connected.

how come it
feels so weird
to think about
sex

31   How come it feels so weird to think about sex?

There could be several reasons for feeling strange when you think about sex. Some people find the idea of sex especially interesting. It makes them feel excited and tingly. Others might not want to imagine people they know—like their own parents—having sex. As well, our cultures have developed a lot of hang-ups about sex so sometimes people talk about sex or behave in ways that make you feel uncomfortable. These things can combine to create a weird feeling. It definitely helps to have a close friend, or your parents or someone you trust, to talk with about these feelings.

Can
children
be gay?

32 Can children be gay?

People may only become aware at puberty whether they are gay or not. Some people know very early on, but others don't realize until they're adults that they love people of their own sex. If two teenagers of the same sex like being together, hugging and sharing their most private secrets, that doesn't mean they're gay. They might just be great best friends.

Sexual identity—that is, how you think of your own sexual feelings and who you are attracted to—isn't just about being gay or heterosexual. There is a whole spectrum of different ways to feel and be.

what does
sex feel like?

33 What does sex feel like?

Sex can feel very different each time. Sometimes it tingles all over and gets very exciting. Sometimes sex is very gentle and quiet, with caresses and soft kisses. Sometimes it may seem more like a wrestling match, or it can feel like a rollercoaster ride. People can have all kinds of intense emotions during sex. The experience is different for every person.

Can people die having sex?

34 Can people die having sex?

Sex can be pretty exciting. The heart beats faster, muscles tense up and the blood pressure rises. Some people say that sex can be as exhausting as a competitive sport. Still, our bodies are built for it. It's incredibly rare for someone to die in the act of having sex. Perhaps if they were already sick or had a weak heart, the exertion during sex might be too great and the person could die. But this hardly ever happens.

What makes
Sex fun?

35 What makes sex fun?

When people are attracted to each other, they want to be as physically close as possible.
They kiss and caress one another. Sex is like an adventure. There are unexplored places all over the body, and familiar places to visit again and again. Sometimes one person lets another take the lead, and sometimes they race through together. Sex can make us feel emotionally close to someone. All that can be a lot of fun!

Sex is fun when the people having sex feel comfortable, happy and safe.

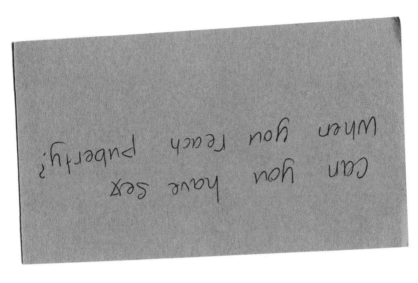

can you have sex
when you reach puberty?

36 Can you have sex when you reach puberty?

Many teenagers have their first boyfriend or girlfriend after they reach puberty. As people grow more in love, the desire to be physically closer grows, too. Some have sex for the first time as teenagers; others wait until they are older. The right time is something each person learns and decides for themselves. And then, of course, they find out what the other person wants as well.

Different cultures and countries have different laws about when people are considered old enough to freely agree to have sex—this is called the "age of consent." Laws about sex between people of different ages prevent older partners from pressuring teenagers into having sex before they are ready.

is it bad to have kids when you are a teenager?

37 Is it bad to have kids when you're a teenager?

Very occasionally you might hear of a young teenage girl who has a baby. This may have been because she had sexual intercourse with someone of her own age. This is a difficult situation. She and the baby's father are still young, and many of their opportunities for growing and learning are much more limited when they have to take care of a baby, so it has a big effect on their future plans. Sometimes the teenagers' parents take responsibility for the baby and help to raise it.

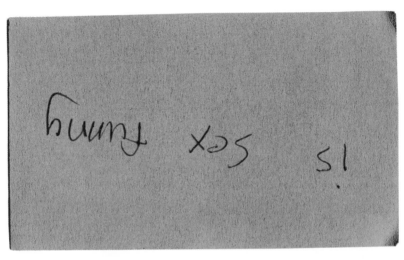

Is Sex funny

HIHI HOHOHO HUHU HAHA

38 Is sex funny?

For many people, sex is about cuddling and fooling around with one another. It feels good to be very close to another person. Sex can be funny. But it can also be much more. Happy, sad, boring, exciting—as varied as people's feelings.

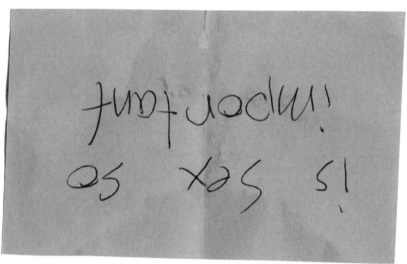

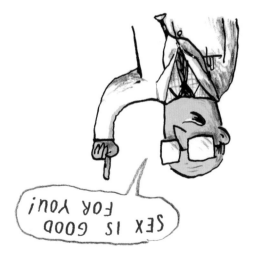

39 Is sex so important?

Sex isn't important for everyone. There are many people who never or hardly ever have sex and are perfectly content. For others, it's very important, and there are many reasons why.

Some reasons people have sex:
- it's fun
- it's good for them
- they want to feel close to the person they love
- they feel like it
- it lets them show how they feel about someone
- they're looking for excitement
- they want to have a child together.

And there are many other reasons.

It's always important that both people want to have sex with each other and that no one feels forced into it.

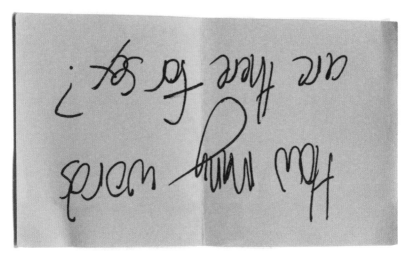

40 How many words are there for sex?

Think about how many you already know. You'll come up with plenty!

- Words that sound quite technical, such as *sexual intercourse*.
- Words that actually describe something else, like *sleeping together* or *going all the way*.
- Swear words that some people don't like to hear or use.
- Funny words like *bonking* or *rumpy pumpy*.
- Silly terms like *a bit of nooky*.
- Other terms like *making love* or *doing it*.

There are words for sex in every language in the world. And people are always coming up with new ones.

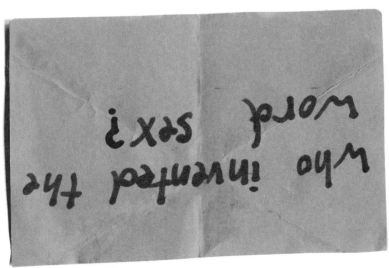

41 Who invented the word sex?

Nobody knows who invented the word. It probably just came about over time. It's actually a very old word from the Latin *sexus*, meaning gender, as in male or female, so it didn't necessarily have anything to do with sleeping together or sexual intercourse. These days we use the word gender differently, too. It refers to a broader idea than the biological sex a person is born with. Gender refers to a whole spectrum of ways people can feel about and present themselves—trans, female, gender fluid, male, bigender, and more...

42 Who was the first person to have sex?

The first person to have sex was also the first person to exist. We can't answer this question more precisely because we don't know exactly who the first humans were, but they lived on the earth more than three million years ago. Humans evolved from animals. They also had sex to reproduce. The earliest humans were people with feelings and needs, just like us. They probably fell in love and got together, and they definitely had sex.

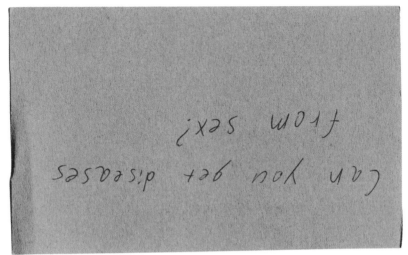

Can you get diseases
from sex?

43 Can you get diseases from sex?

If someone with a cold or flu coughs on you any time, you can get infected with that virus or bacteria. During sex you are physically close to someone else and viruses or bacteria can be passed from one body to another. So you can get infected by someone who already carries a disease.

Particular infections can be passed on through bodily fluids when people have sex. These are called STIs (sexually transmitted infections). All of these are unpleasant; some are dangerous and have serious consequences. A condom provides good protection against viruses or infections being passed from one body to another. People who are healthy and only have sex with a partner they know well and trust usually do not have to protect themselves against STIs during sex.

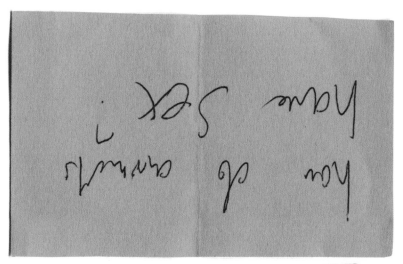

44　How do animals have sex?

Almost all animals reproduce by having sex. How they do it varies. All mammals do it the same way: the male climbs onto the female and pushes his penis into her vagina. It's a bit different for birds. There's no penis or vagina. Instead, they have an opening called the cloaca that sticks out during fertilization. When the male sits on the female bird, seeds flow into the female's cloaca. The fertilized egg is eventually laid in the nest and hatched.

Even dinosaurs had sex. Researchers believe the male dinosaur climbed onto the female to mate. It's likely some dinosaurs had a penis or vagina just like mammals. Others probably reproduced like birds, through their cloacas.

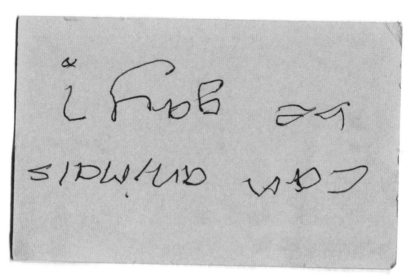

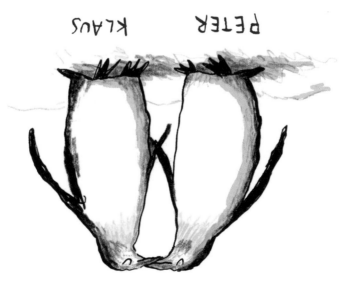

45 Can animals be gay?

Animal researchers have observed that in many species, males mate with males or females with females. It might be for quick sex, or it might last a few months or for the animals' lifetime. As with humans, sex in animals can differ widely. For example, there are male penguin couples that incubate eggs and raise their offspring together, or female monkeys that enjoy having sex together. Just like humans, animals have sex not only to produce offspring, but because it's fun and gives them pleasure.

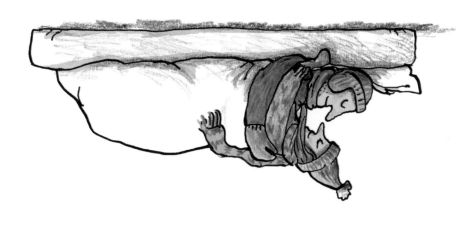

do you have to
be naked
to have sex?

46 Do you have to be naked to have sex?

No! No one has to do anything during sex.

- Many people are naked during sex so they can get physically closer to one another.

- Some people keep their socks on so their feet don't get cold.

- Some people have sex so quickly there's no time to take off all their clothes.

- Some people put on special clothes to make themselves extra attractive to the other person.

Each person does it the way they like. There are no rules except that each person must want to have sex.

How do a man
and a woman
have sex?

47 How do a man and a woman have sex?

"Having sex" can mean many things—it's all about kissing, caressing, cuddling and much more. It's about people wanting to be very close and touch each other so their bodies feel all tingly.

If a woman and a man both want to have sexual intercourse, once the man's penis gets very hard and the woman's vagina gets wet, they slide the penis into the vagina. Each movement back and forth makes the tingling sensation stronger until it suddenly comes to a quivery climax, called an orgasm. It feels a bit like being on a swing, getting higher and higher, until at the highest point there's a feeling of happy release.

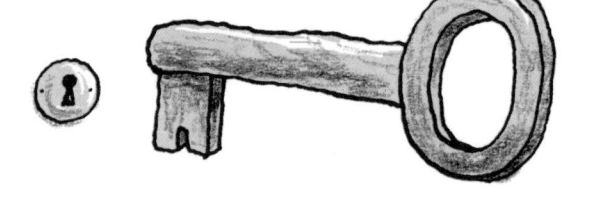

48

How do you have sex if the penis is too big and the vagina too small?

48 How do you have sex if the penis is too big and the vagina too small?

In most cases this is not a problem when adults have sex. The vagina is a very supple passage that can stretch pretty wide. (Even a baby can pass through it during birth.) Besides, the vagina automatically gets moist when a woman is in the mood for sex. This makes it easier for even a large penis to slide into it. The most important thing is for everyone to communicate—and to stop if someone is not comfortable.

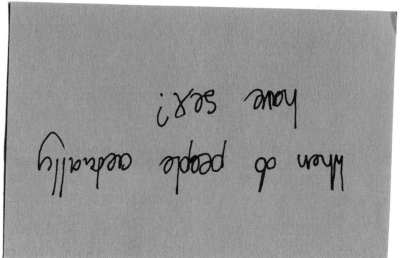

When do people actually have sex?

49   When do people actually have sex?

Sex is an intimate business. People usually choose times and places when they won't be disturbed—perhaps when children are sleeping or spending the night away or are at school. Or they may meet in a completely different place. Adults have plenty of ideas!

If you accidently come upon people having sex, you are probably bursting in on a moment when they would prefer to be alone. They're having sex. So, shhhh! Best to close the door again quietly.

What is homosexual?

50 What is homosexual?

Homo means "the same." So homosexual means feeling sexual with someone of the same sex. *Gay* and *queer* are more commonly used words, and gay women are also called *lesbians*.

For some people, their sexual identity becomes clear quite early in their lives. Others might take a while to work it out or feel differently at different times in their lives. Every person is different. There are left- and right-handed people, athletic and non-athletic, shy and loud—and all the variations in between. Sexual identity has just as many variations. The main thing is that everyone feels good being the way they are.

What does LGBT mean

51 What does LGBT mean?

People are different and people love differently. LGBT and variations like LGBTQ+ are abbreviations for people who live and love differently from the male–female combination (heterosexual).

L stands for "lesbian": women who love women.

G stands for "gay": anyone who loves people of the same sex as they are, especially men who love men.

B stands for "bisexual": women who love women and men, or men who love men and women.

T stands for "trans": women who were seen as boys at birth because of their physical characteristics or men who were seen as girls at birth because of their physical characteristics.

Q stands for "queer": an umbrella term that describes many sexual identities other than heterosexuality.

And + to show there are many different ways to live and love.

How often do people have sex?

52   How often do people have sex?

Basically, people can have as much sex as they find is good for them. Some people like having sex quite often, others only once a year, some not at all. People don't always feel the same way. New lovers might have sex frequently at first, then later find it's not so important to them as a couple. Or someone may discover great sex for the first time when they're a grandma or grandpa. Everyone is different.

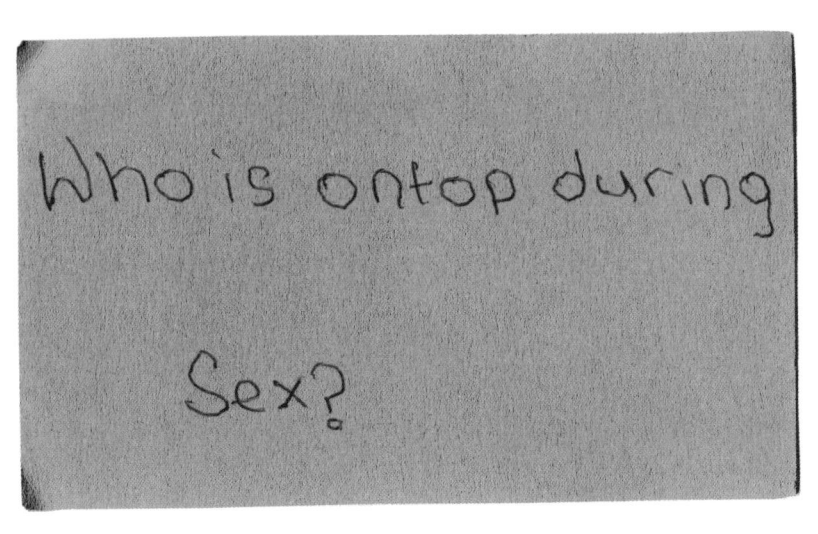

Who is ontop during Sex?

53 Who is on top during sex?

People have many ideas about how they can have sex. Either partner can be on top, and there are no rules. Some people take turns, others always do the same thing. And there are other positions, too. Not just above and below, but front and behind or left and right, standing, sitting, lying down—people work out together what they want to do and how.

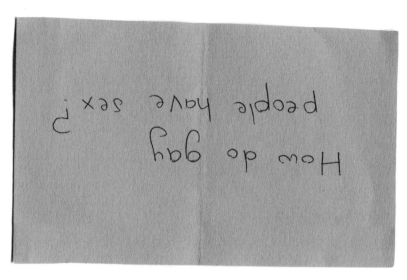

How do gay people have sex?

54 How do gay people have sex?

Sex can happen without a penis going into a vagina. There's a lot more to sex than you might imagine. The people having sex touch each other in sensitive areas and give each other pleasure to bring about the thrilling sensation called orgasm. Lesbian women, gay men and trans men and women have sex just like all people who are in love or want to feel and touch each another. The only difference is that sex between gay people will not produce a child.

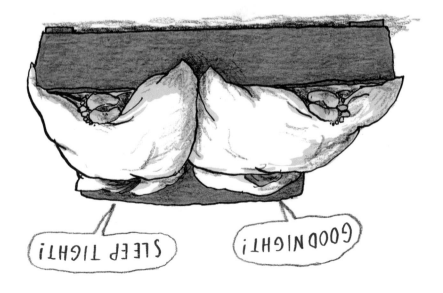

55 What happens if you don't feel like having sex?

Hopefully, nothing! Because if you don't feel like it, then you shouldn't do it. It's always okay to say no. You can simply tell the other person that you don't feel like it or don't want to. It is the responsibility of the person who wants to have sex to check that the other person really wants to as well. Adults don't always want to have sex. Sometimes they're too tired or sad or in a bad mood, or they just don't feel like it.

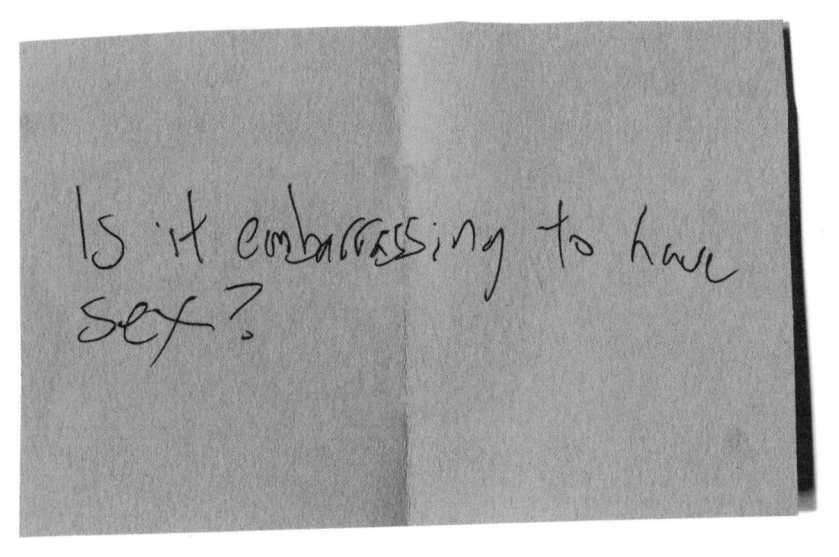

Is it embarrassing to have sex?

56   Is it embarrassing to have sex?

If people trust or love each other, it's not usually embarrassing for them to have sex. If they communicate what they're feeling and respect each other, there's nothing to be embarrassed about. They know what the other person is feeling and how they like to be touched.

But sex can also feel awkward, perhaps because you show a different side of yourself during sex. You're often naked, sometimes sweaty, sometimes moaning with pleasure, and you're not always completely in control. Sometimes it helps to tell a good joke or two afterwards, so things don't feel so weird. But most important is to make sure your sex partners are caring and respectful toward you.

Do you have sex
before or after
you wedding?

57 Do you have sex before or after your wedding?

Most people today find it normal to have sex before their wedding. This is mainly because the desire for sex often comes sooner than the desire to marry. Many people also think it's good to try sex and practice a bit. Fifty years ago it was usual for couples to wait until after the wedding to have sex. At least, most couples tried to do so. Certainly there are people all over the world who want—or are expected—to get married before they have sex for the first time, but there are many other people who never marry at all.

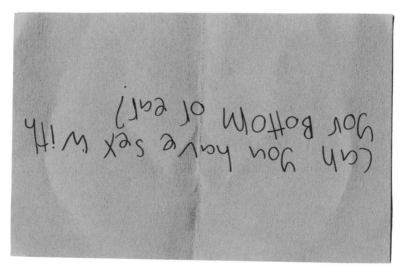

58 Can you have sex with your bottom or ear?

Having sex doesn't just mean having contact with a penis or a vagina. Sex includes stroking, hugging, kissing, feeling comfortable together and much more—whatever feels good. Buttocks and ears are certainly parts of the body with many nerve cells under the skin and are particularly sensitive to touch.

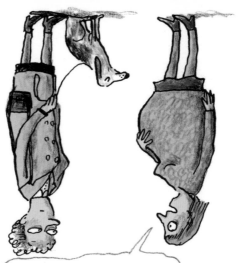

59   Can you have children without having sex?

For a baby to begin growing, an egg cell must be fertilized by a sperm cell. Most of the time this happens during sex. But sometimes the sperm can reach the egg a different way, such as in a laboratory under a microscope. The fertilized egg is then implanted into the woman's body—this is called *in vitro fertilization*. Or the sperm cells may be put directly into the woman's body using a kind of syringe. This is called *artificial insemination*. People can also become parents by adopting children.

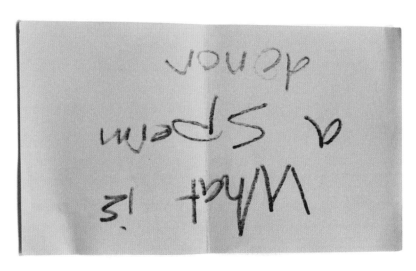

60   What is a sperm donor?

This is a person who donates or sells their sperm. The sperm cells are collected and frozen and kept in a sperm bank for medical research or for couples who can't have a child without medical help. If someone wishes to be a sperm donor, they are first thoroughly checked to make sure they don't have any diseases and their sperm is of very good quality.

Informally, a sperm donor might be someone who helps out a friend—they might donate sperm to enable someone they know to become pregnant.

Do babies get made
every time you have sex?

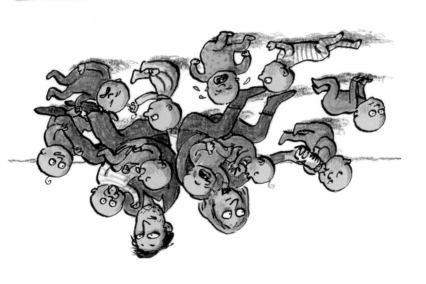

61 Do babies get made every time you have sex?

No! A child is formed only when a sperm cell and an egg cell merge. Then the woman gets pregnant. But that doesn't happen every time people have sex. Sometimes the egg isn't ready, or the sperm cells don't reach the egg because the people are using contraception. There are many different reasons why a woman might not get pregnant during sex. Most people have sex much more often than they produce children—because they like having sex!

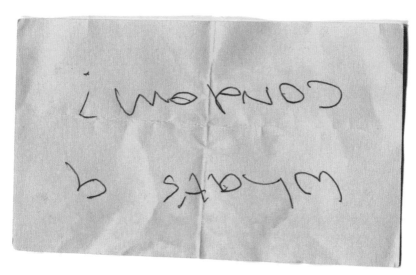

62 What's a condom?

A condom can be used if a woman doesn't want to become pregnant or to protect against infections that can be passed on during sex.

A condom is made from very thin latex or polyurethane and looks a bit like a long balloon before it's blown up. External condoms fit over the stiff penis and internal condoms fit inside the vagina. The semen that comes out of the penis during sex is caught in the condom and doesn't go into the other person's body. Because every penis is different, external condoms come in different sizes.

Stopping sperm and egg cells from combining to make a baby is called *contraception* or *birth control*. Protecting yourself from infections during sex is *safer sex*.

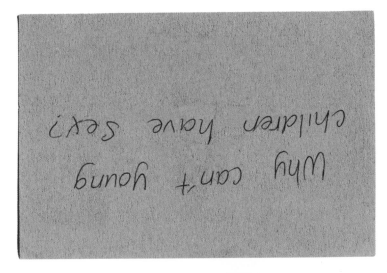

Why can't young children have sex?

WE'D MAKE A PERFECT COUPLE.

63 Why can't young children have sex?

Children don't yet desire sex or sexual intercourse and their bodies are not ready for sex. It's only later when you're a teenager, or later still as an adult, that you feel the desire for sex. But many kids do like to cuddle or tickle one another under the blankets. There are plenty of different ways to show affection for each other. Some children like to touch their own bodies when they are alone and feel sexual pleasure. This is fine and a good way to get to know your own body and how and where you like to be touched. These are things you can share when you are older and ready to be sexual with other people.

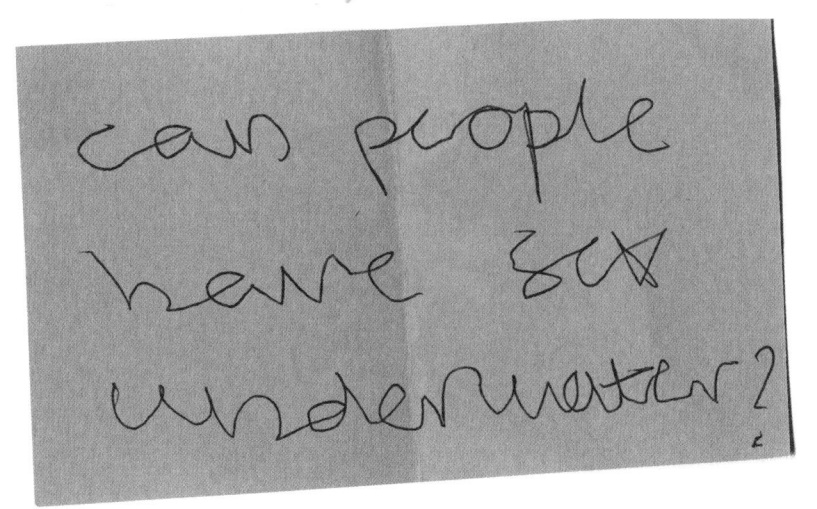

64 Can people have sex underwater?

Yes, that's possible. If they can hold their breath long enough! In fact, people can have sex anywhere—under the dining-room table, on the beach, on the roof of the garage, in the bathtub, in the car, between the shelves in the basement. The main thing is that they feel they're in the right place with the right person. And that they're somewhere private so other people won't feel upset or awkward.

Why do people
Moan and Groan
during sex?

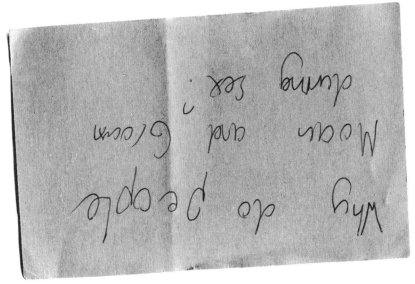

DID YOU HAVE
A NIGHTMARE
LAST NIGHT?

65 Why do people moan and groan during sex?

People don't always make noise during sex. For some people sex is such a wonderful and exciting activity that they groan or even scream. It doesn't mean they're hurt. On the contrary, you could compare sex to a rollercoaster ride, when you shout from sheer joy and excitement.

What is
m+s+u+b+t+i+on?

66   What's masturbation?

Many people find it exciting and pleasurable to touch sensitive parts of their own body, such as the breasts, penis, clitoris and vulva, stroking them again and again. This touching is called masturbation. The delicious feeling can grow and become more and more intense until it might peak in a little explosion of happiness called an orgasm. With older people, semen comes out of the penis or the vagina becomes wet.

Everyone is different. Some people masturbate often, while others never want to. In any case, masturbation is something children should do alone.

It's good and completely normal to want to get to know your body better.

WHAT IS
PORN?

67 What is porn?

Porn is the abbreviation for the word pornography. These are films, books or magazines that show people during sexual activity. Some adults watch porn for themselves to get sexual pleasure. Mostly, the sex shown in pornography has nothing to do with real life. Actors in pornographic films have often had surgery to change their bodies and they may be filmed doing things that most people wouldn't do or enjoy in real life because they would be painful or uncomfortable. A lot of pornography also treats violence as normal or shows women being treated badly. It is illegal for children and teenagers to watch porn or be shown it by adults.

what is sexy?

89

68 What is sexy?

If you call someone "really sexy," it means you think they're fantastic and attractive. You usually mean that they look good to you or have a certain magnetism. Even clothing can be called sexy, if it clings to the body, for example, or is very short or has a low neckline. Everyone has a different idea of "sexy." Some people find a gap between the front teeth sexy. For others it may be a particular voice, or a small mole above the lip. People also use the word sexy to describe anything at all that they like.

69

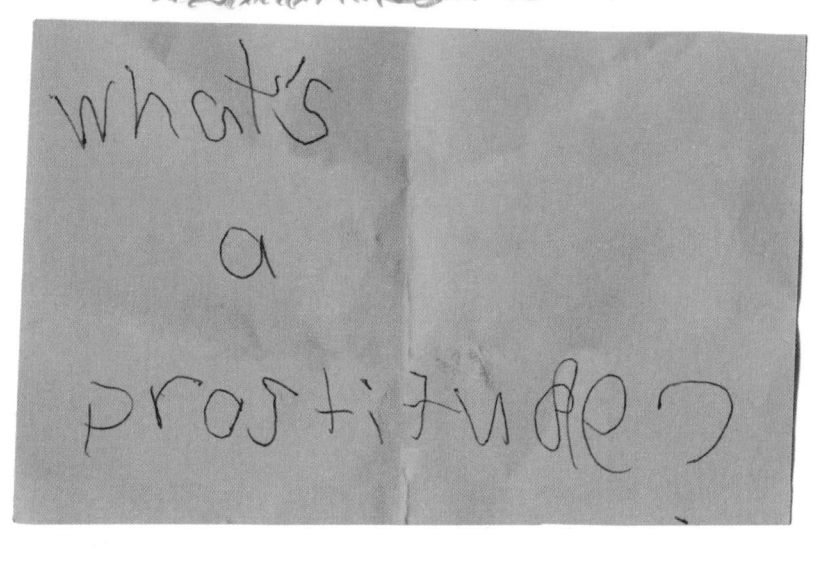

what's a prostitude?

69 What's a prostitute?

A prostitute is a sex worker: someone who is paid to have sex. Some people do this work willingly. Others find themselves trapped in the job for various reasons including poverty or a lack of other options. Prostitution is illegal in some countries.

What goes on in a sex shop?

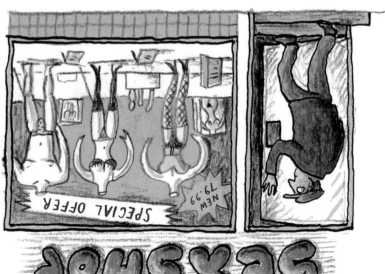

70   What goes on in a sex shop?

This is a shop where you can buy things related to sex, including underwear, condoms, things to use during sex, and movies and books that show sex. Some of these movies and books are also called pornography or porn. Some adults watch porn for sexual pleasure, although most of the sex shown in porn has nothing to do with real life. Only adults are allowed to go into sex shops.

How many people have
already had sex?

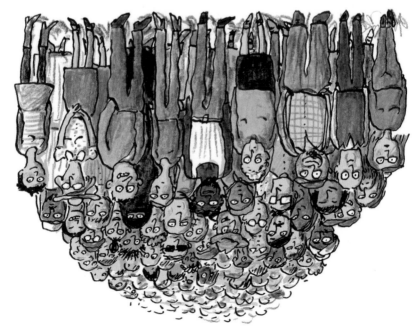

How many people have already had sex?

Nobody has to keep track of who they have had sex with. Even though such a list might be useful to answer this question!

Having sex is part of being human. Otherwise we wouldn't all be here. People have sex because they feel like it, because it makes them happy, or because they want to have children... Most adults have had sex, but there are also people who never have sex in their lives. Some people don't want to and never will. So far, around 110 billion people have lived on the earth. Even if you subtract the few who have never had sex, that's a huge number.

What is
Sexual harassment?

72   What is sexual harassment?

If someone harasses you, they're annoying you.
You can't shake them off, and you feel upset. You
probably know the feeling.

Sexual harassment goes further. For example, if
someone keeps following you and telling you how
sexy you are. They might not stop even when they
realize you don't like it. Someone might talk to you
about your body or sex for no reason, and that
makes you uncomfortable. Or show you pictures of
people naked or having sex. Or touch your body in
a way that you don't like or that frightens you.

Sexual harassment can happen online or in person.
You can experience sexual harassment no matter
your gender or sexual orientation, and it's never
your fault—the person in the wrong is the person
who harasses you. Harassment is not about what
the other person intends, it's about how they make
you feel.

It's important to pay attention to your feelings. If
you feel uncomfortable, it's a good idea to tell a
trusted adult about it. They can help you stop the
person who is sexually harassing you.

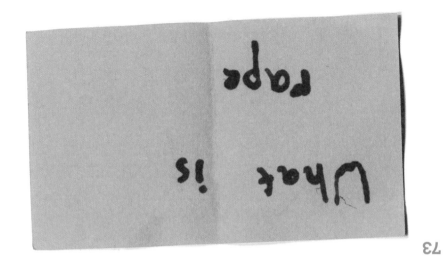

73 What is rape?

Rape is when a person is forced to have sex against their will. This is a terrible thing to experience. Sex is very personal for each one of us, and everyone can and should decide about it for themselves. No one has the right to force someone else to have sex. This is a criminal offence.

When we talk about sex we often talk about the idea of "consent." It is important that anyone involved in any kind of sexual activity wants to be doing what they are doing.

If anyone forces you into sexual activity without your consent, you should tell an adult you trust as soon as you can.

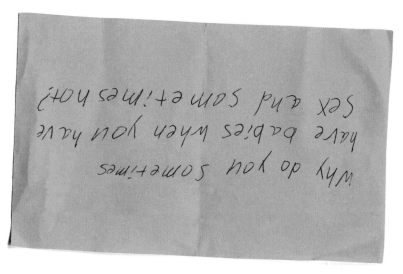

Why do you sometimes
have babies when you have
sex and sometimes not?

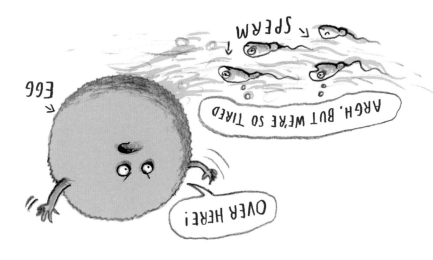

74 Why do you sometimes have babies when you have sex and sometimes not?

Many different things have to happen at the same time for a woman to get pregnant.

- In the woman's ovary, there must be a mature egg that jumps into the fallopian tube. It's there for only a few hours every month.
- During this time, sperm cells must be nearby to fertilize the egg.
- The sperm must be able to swim fast enough.
- The fertilized egg needs to find a good spot to stay in the lining of the uterus.

If just one of these things doesn't happen, no baby will grow inside the uterus.

If a couple wants to be sure they won't have a baby, they must use contraception (such as a condom) to prevent the sperm and egg from getting together.

Sometimes, people do everything to try to get the egg and sperm together, but the woman still doesn't get pregnant. For those couples, who want to have a child, every month brings sad news.

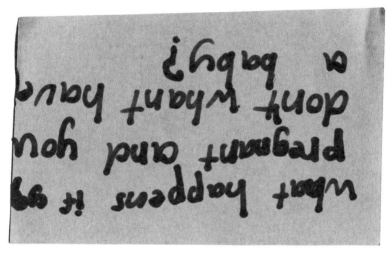

What happens if you pregnant and you dont whant have a baby?

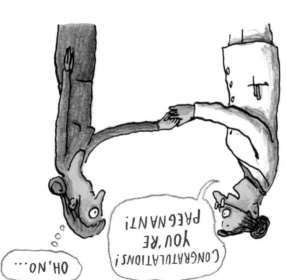

75 What happens if you're pregnant and you don't want to have a baby?

Sometimes a woman becomes pregnant but feels she cannot have a child. She might feel unable to look after a child properly, have worries of her own, or there may be other reasons. Then she's anxious and sad about her pregnancy instead of being happy.

It's important that this woman has someone she can talk to. This could be her partner, a close friend or a doctor. The woman might decide to let other parents adopt or foster her baby so they can take care of it. Or she might choose to end the pregnancy with an abortion (a medical procedure). In the early stages this is possible with a doctor's help.

No matter what a woman does in this situation, the decision is very difficult for her.

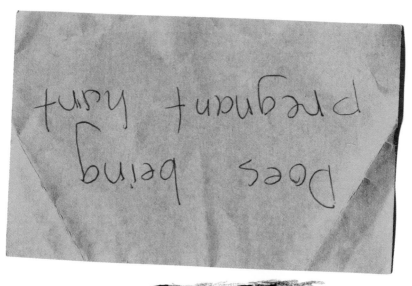

Does being
Pregnant hurt?

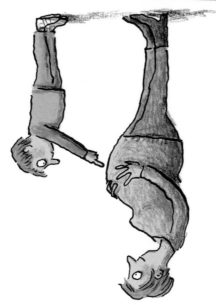

76 Does being pregnant hurt?

No, being pregnant doesn't hurt. However, sometimes a woman finds things aren't quite as easy with a child in her uterus. In the first few weeks or months she might feel sick at times. Her body keeps changing as well. Her breasts get bigger and her belly gets bigger as the baby grows. She might get backaches or become exhausted just climbing the stairs. A mother might feel the child move and kick in her belly, and that can feel pleasant or a bit uncomfortable.

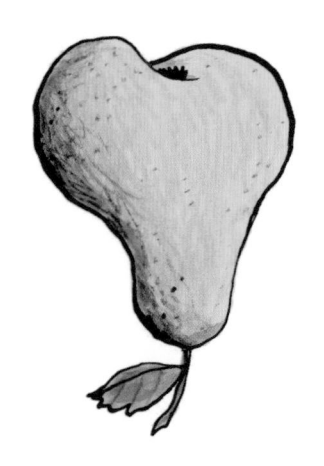

How big is
a uterus?

77 How big is a uterus?

The uterus, or womb, is about the size and shape of a small upside-down pear. It has a thick muscle layer. In pregnancy the uterus can stretch so there's room for a baby to grow until it's ready to be born. By then the uterus is almost as big as a watermelon.

Whats the most children
You can have?

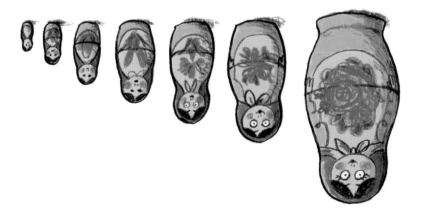

What's the most children you can have?

About 300 years ago, a woman living in Russia was pregnant 27 times and had a total of 69 children: sixteen pairs of twins, seven sets of triplets and four sets of quadruplets. That is the record.

A man can have many, many more children during his lifetime than a woman. He doesn't get pregnant and have to wait nine months for a child to grow inside his body. So a man could have sex with many different women who become pregnant from his many sperm. The Moroccan prince Mulai Ismail is said to have had more than 850 children with 500 different women.

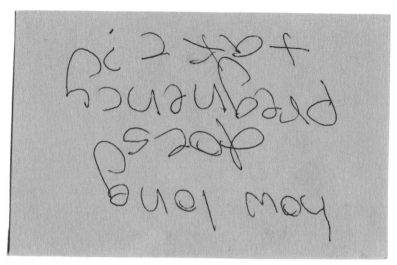

how long does a false pregnancy last?

79   How long does pregnancy take?

Pregnancy lasts about nine months or, to be more specific, 40 weeks. During this time, the tiny sperm cell and egg cell join and develop into a human being ready to be born. Sometimes the baby comes into the world a little earlier or a few days later than expected. You can't determine the exact time of birth.

what happens to
babies when pregnant
women smoke?

80 What happens to babies when pregnant women smoke?

Smoking is bad for you. That's true for both the pregnant mother and the baby in her womb. Toxins in smoke get into the mother's bloodstream and are passed to the baby through the placenta and umbilical cord. This can prevent the baby from getting enough oxygen and nutrients, and stop it from developing properly. Often these babies are especially small at birth. They might have breathing problems or be more likely to become sick as children. It's certainly best for a mother not to smoke during pregnancy.

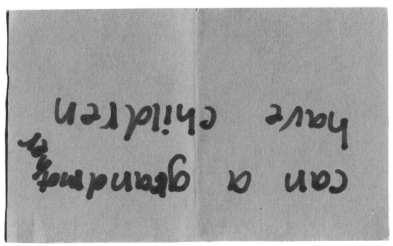

can a grandmother have children

81 Can a grandmother have children?

That depends on how old the grandmother is and whether she is still producing eggs. During puberty, females begin to regularly produce mature eggs. This continues for many years until, at some point between 45 and 55 years, their hormones change and the eggs stop maturing. Then a woman can no longer have children. This time of change is called menopause. So if a grandmother is still relatively young, she can become pregnant. Then her baby might be the aunt or uncle of her grandchild, as crazy as that sounds!

It's different with males. Their bodies begin to make sperm cells during puberty and never stop, although they make fewer as they get older. That's why even old men can become fathers.

can gay people have (an) children

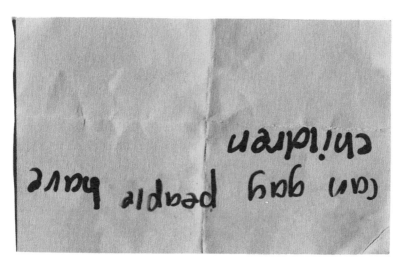

82

82 Can gay people have children?

Two people of the same sex can't have children by having sex. To make a baby you need a sperm cell and an egg cell. Couples who don't have both of these need to find someone who can give them whichever cell they are missing. Some lesbian couples will get sperm from a man they know. Or they can buy sperm. Gay couples might ask a woman to have a child for them. Gay or lesbian couples can also adopt a child or add a foster child to their family.

why do rebel sometimes lose a baby?

83 Why do people sometimes lose a baby?

Not every woman gives birth to a child after nine months of pregnancy. Sometimes there are problems and the child doesn't grow properly in the womb. Then it dies before it even comes into the world. Sometimes a child is born too early, when it's too small to live outside the womb and the baby dies. For parents who've been looking forward so much to having a child, these situations are very hard. But most women can get pregnant again and bring a healthy baby into the world.

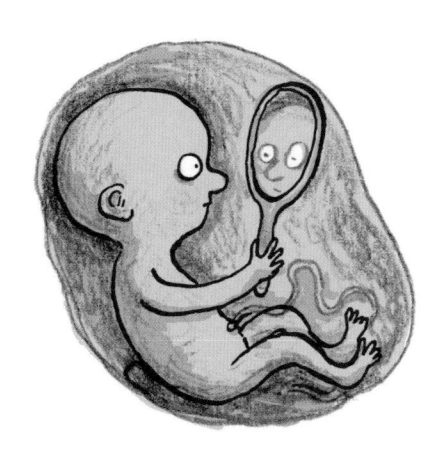

What do you look like

before you are born?

84   What do you look like before you are born?

Each child starts off as a small cluster of cells, which grows bigger and bigger and looks more and more like a person with a head, body, arms and legs. There are photos of babies at various stages inside the mother's uterus. In the first months, they look like aliens! But at the end of the pregnancy, the baby is complete and ready to be born. At worst, it's a bit wrinkly from being in amniotic fluid and tightly folded inside the womb.

how long before
you know it's a
girl of a boy?

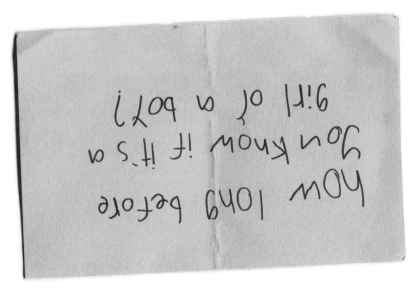

85 How long before you know if it's a girl or a boy?

About halfway through the pregnancy (in the fourth to fifth month), a doctor can be pretty sure about the biological sex of the baby. With the help of an ultrasound machine, you can see inside the uterus. If you're lucky and the child is in a good position, you can see testicles and a penis or the vaginal labia between the legs.

The biological sex of the child is set at the moment of fertilization, when the sperm merges with the egg. It's completely a matter of chance what the combination will produce. Some babies are intersex—they have sexual parts associated with both males and females.

How a person feels inside about their gender isn't known until the person can and wants to tell others.

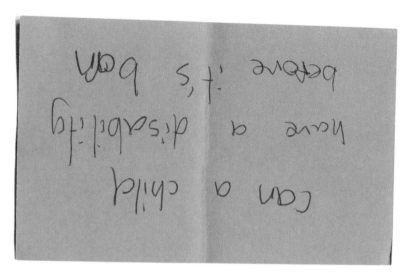

can a child
have a disability
before it's born

98

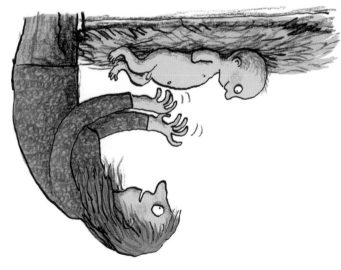

86 Can a child have a disability before it's born?

Very few babies are born with a disability, and there are many different kinds of disability. There are children who can't see or hear, children who can't control their movements, children who don't develop the way healthy babies do, and many more. These difficulties can be inherited, or there might be complications in the womb so the baby doesn't develop as it should have. Occasionally a baby gets short of oxygen during birth, and this can also lead to a disability.

Some disabilities begin while the baby is still growing inside the mother and some develop later in life or are because of other things that happen to someone. Many people have disabilities you can't see immediately.

87

what do babies eat
when they're
inside the womb?
Dose the mother
have to eat more?

87   What do babies eat when they're inside the womb? Does the mother have to eat more?

A baby in the uterus can't eat yet. The mother supplies everything it needs. All the important nutrients go directly into its small body through the umbilical cord. The baby doesn't have to chew or digest. It just has to grow and develop. Sometimes it drinks amniotic fluid. Whatever the mother eats reaches the baby as well. So a pregnant woman should eat as healthy a diet as possible. And she should eat a bit more than usual, too, because the growing baby needs many nutrients.

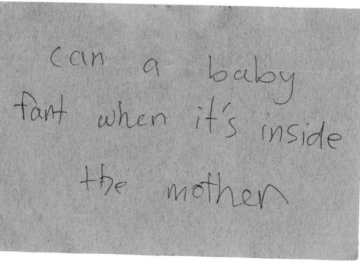

88 Can a baby fart when it's inside the mother?

No, it can't, because its stomach and intestines aren't working yet. That means no air forms in the baby's intestines to be farted out. But the child can drink amniotic fluid. It can also pee.

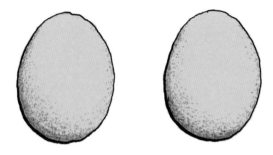

89

why do some twins look so much alike

89 Why do some twins look so much alike?

Some twins look like the spitting image of each other. That's because they both came from the same fertilized egg cell. While most eggs develop into one child, when a fertilized egg cell splits in two, you get identical twins. Same sex, same hair colour, same nose shape and so on. Sometimes you can't tell them apart except by comparing their fingerprints.

There are also fraternal twins who don't look exactly alike. They develop when two egg cells are released at the same time (usually there is only one) and are fertilized by two sperm cells. Fraternal twins can be quite different or quite similar, just as with other siblings.

90 Why does giving birth hurt so much?

During birth, the muscles of the uterus contract over and over to help push the baby out. These contractions really hurt and can be very stressful for the mother, especially towards the end. But the mother is not totally at the mercy of these pains. She can endure them by breathing deeply through the contractions and moving around in between them. If it gets too intense, there are other things doctors and midwives can do to help with the pain. At the same time, the mother knows that the pain will come to an end. And then she can finally hold her baby in her arms!

91

Why does the woman have to push when the baby comes?

91 Why does the woman have to push when the baby comes?

To be born, the baby has a cramped and exhausting journey to make. At first the muscles of the uterus contract again and again, pushing the baby's head towards the opening of the vagina. These are the contractions. When the birth gets closer the pains bring the urge to bear down. Most women feel the need to push very hard. They want to get the baby out! It feels a bit like sitting on the toilet and having to push out something the size of a pumpkin.

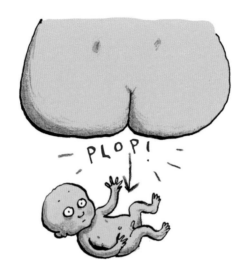

Can you have a baby out of your Bottom?

92 Can you have a baby out of your bottom?

No! In humans and all mammals, the anus is the end of the intestines, where only excrement comes out—in other words, poop. A baby grows in a woman's uterus. There is no connection between the uterus and the anus. The only exit from the uterus is the vaginal opening.

93

Does the vagina bleed when a baby is born?

93 Does the vagina bleed when a baby is born?

Most of a birth is not particularly bloody. The child has to be squeezed through the narrow passage of the vagina, and sometimes amniotic fluid and a little blood or bloody mucous comes with it. The vagina and surrounding areas can get hurt when the baby is born but with proper care they should be okay.

After the mother has given birth to the baby, she pushes the placenta out of the vagina. The placenta is the lining of the uterus that protected and nourished the baby as it grew. Up until the birth, this organ provided the baby with blood and nutrients, but now it is no longer needed. It can look a bit bloody, too.

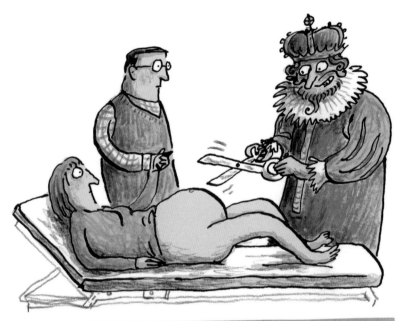

94

What is a
caesarian section?

94 What is a cesarean section?

If a baby can't be delivered through the vagina,
perhaps because it's upside down or very big,
a cesarean section is done. In this operation
the abdomen and uterus are cut open a bit. The
surgeon lifts the baby from the abdomen, cuts
the umbilical cord, and sews the mother's uterus
and abdomen closed again. The name cesarean
comes from the belief that the first person to
be born this way was an ancestor of the Roman
emperor, Julius Caesar.

95

How long dose
it take fore a
baby to be born?

95 How long does it take for a baby to be born?

A birth can take a long time. Sometimes a woman has contractions for many, many hours, and it can take more than a day for the baby to finally be born. But there are also very fast births, when the baby comes out of the vagina after a short time. Sometimes this even happens in the car on the way to the hospital! You can never tell how long a birth will take.

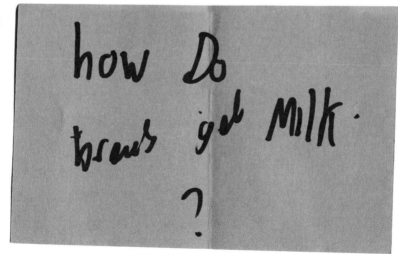

96 How do breasts get milk?

Breasts contain nerves, fatty tissue and mammary glands that branch out in small passages, or ducts, through the breasts to the nipple. The mammary glands are small and unnoticeable until they're needed. When a woman becomes pregnant, the milk ducts get bigger and form more branches. But it's only when the child is born and sucks hard on the breast that the ducts produce milk to nourish the baby.

Are kids born smart?

97 Are kids born smart?

Most children are born with a brain that works well. The brain is the basis for being smart. From the very first hours of life, babies are always learning new things, and their brains are very busy. So children don't arrive in the world smart. But they get smarter as they learn, see and experience more things.

Why is every person different, and why do some people look alike

98 Why is every person different, and why do some people look alike?

There's only one person exactly like you in this world! That's because, at the time of fertilization, a particular egg merged with a particular sperm cell. A millisecond earlier and it would have been a different sperm cell, and a different human would have been born. Your parents' egg and sperm cells contain specific genetic information that is passed on from them, which may result in, say, blue eyes, a crooked nose or big feet. That's why family members often look alike.

Is it better to be a kid or a grown up?

99   Is it better to be a kid or a grownup?

A child might answer that it's better to be a grownup. That way you can decide for yourself when to go to bed, which movies you can watch and how often you brush your teeth. It sounds like paradise! But an adult might think back to the good times when they didn't have to organize and decide on everything themselves, when they could run around freely and make noise and play and forget about time. It's best to remember how it feels to be a kid. Then you can more or less have it both ways when you grow up.

Tell me

This edition first published in 2019 by Gecko Press
PO Box 9335, Wellington 6141, New Zealand
info@geckopress.com

English-language edition © Gecko Press Ltd 2019
Translation © Shelley Tanaka 2019

Originally published as *Klär Mich Auf* © 2014 Klett Kinderbuch
GmbH, Leipzig, Germany

The translation of this book was supported by a grant from
the Goethe-Institut which is funded by the German Ministry
of Foreign Affairs.

GOETHE
INSTITUT

Gecko Press wishes to thank the teachers, sexuality
educators, parents and children who helped review and edit
the English edition, and the children who handwrote questions
in English. The question What does LGBT mean? was not in
the original book but was asked by children helping to prepare
the English edition.

Edited by Penelope Todd
Cover design and typesetting by Spencer Levine
Printed in China by Everbest Printing Co. Ltd,
an accredited ISO 14001 & FSC-certified printer

ISBN hardback: 978-1-776572-32-8

For more curiously good books, visit geckopress.com